Creatures from
My Bathroom Wall

Creatures from My Bathroom Wall

LAURA BURGESS

TATE PUBLISHING
AND ENTERPRISES, LLC

Published by Tate Publishing & Enterprises, LLC
127 E. Trade Center Terrace | Mustang, Oklahoma 73064 USA
1.888.361.9473 | www.tatepublishing.com

Tate Publishing is committed to excellence in the publishing industry. The company reflects the philosophy established by the founders, based on Psalm 68:11,
"The Lord gave the word and great was the company of those who published it."

Book design copyright © 2014 by Tate Publishing, LLC. All rights reserved.
Cover design by Nikolai Purpura
Interior design by Mary Jean Archival

Published in the United States of America

ISBN: 978-1-63063-221-2
1. Poetry / Subjects & Themes / Inspirational & Religious
2. Poetry / General
13.01.24

Acknowledgments

Praise to my heavenly Father whose limitless creativity created this book, and thanks to my earthly father whose imagination continues to inspire my own.

Author's Note

This book began one day as I was sitting in my bathroom, looking at the sponge painting on the wall. I realized that there was a creature looking back at me, so I reached for my drawing pad and captured him on paper. From then on, creatures were continually appearing and disappearing on that wall. I watched as God used me to capture many of them on paper and then match them with Bible verses. From there, he created the poetry to accompany them.

This book was originally intended to be a book for our family, a celebration of my dad whose imagination has inspired all of us, and an inspiration for my grandchildren, to pass on his legacy. But God had bigger plans.

So we offer it to share with you. I pray that God will provoke your thoughts, tickle your funny bone, and draw you deeper into his presence through his creatures. May we all have eyes to see that which is unseen.

Contents

Laura Burgess

Still

If I could be but perfectly still
And hear the Word of God,
The stars and moon would dance with joy,
For the blessing on me, his child.

> Be still, and know that I am God: I will be exalted among
> the heathen, I will be exalted in the earth.

Psalm 46:10 (KJV)

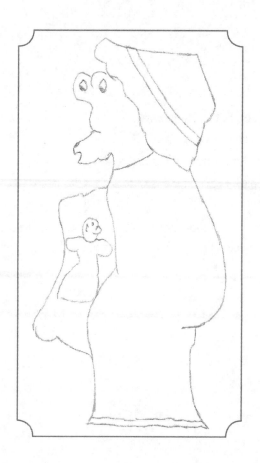

Laura Burgess

Unexpected

Surprised by joy and in delight
She gazed upon the child.
Her gift from God, an orphan lone,
His will to be her own.

> He maketh the barren woman to keep house, and to be
> a joyful mother of children. Praise ye the LORD.
>
> Psalm 113:9 (KJV)

Laura Burgess

Wings

Mount up, mount up! The cry goes out.
Fly high above the stormy sky, and never, ever doubt.
The Lord will guide the trusting ones, and they shall be his own,
To walk and run and fly above, in Christ and him alone.

> But they that wait upon the LORD shall renew their
> strength; they shall mount up with wings as eagles; they
> shall run, and not be weary; and they shall walk, and not
> faint.

> Isaiah 40:31 (KJV)

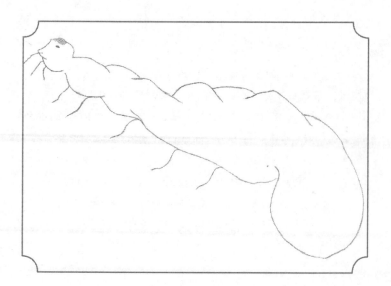

Laura Burgess

Yes

Fear not to obey the Lord, for he will go before,
As he did for Moses in the days of yore.
The key to God's provision
Is your *yes* to his command.
So lift up your head, stretch forth your hand,
And watch his grace expand!

> And they did so; for Aaron stretched out his hand with his rod, and smote the dust of the earth, and it became lice in man, and in beast; all the dust of the land became lice throughout all the land of Egypt.
>
> Exodus 8:17 (KJV)

Laura Burgess

Innumerable

The flying fish, the tiny snail,
The graceful coral strand,
Creations myriad, both great and small,
Designings from his hand,
Proclaim his glory, sing his love,
And bow to his command.

> So is this great and wide sea, wherein are things creeping innumerable, both small and great beasts.
>
> Psalm 104:25 (KJV)

Laura Burgess

Use Me

Pour me out, Lord, let me be
The offering you choose to use,
To speak to hearts, proclaim your love,
And draw us to your throne.

> But even if I am being poured out like a drink offering
> on the sacrifice and service coming from your faith, I
> am glad and rejoice with all of you.

Philippians 2:17 (NIV)

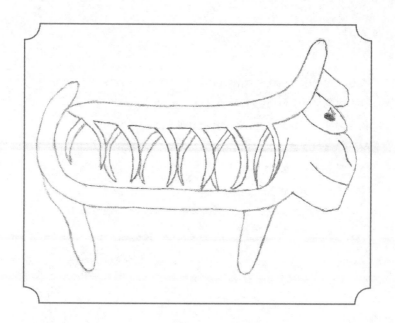

Laura Burgess

Bestirred

The rattling of those old dry bones,
The dryness in one's soul,
The clouded mind, the stubborn will,
All bow to just one rule.

The word of God, so sharp and clear,
Can make the dead man breathe,
So bones, hear this, Jesus lives!
And so will you. Believe!

> O ye dry bones, hear the word of the LORD… and ye shall
> live; and ye shall know that I am the LORD.
>
> Ezekiel 37:4–6 (KJV)

Laura Burgess

Rejoice!

Oh, dance and sing and praise his name!
And let your feet rejoice!
The Lord is good and he is here,
And I must raise my voice.
So sing with me and laugh with joy
And dance with all your might,
For God is pleased to dance with us
And share with us his light!

> O magnify the LORD with me, and let us exalt his name together.
>
> Psalm 34:3 (KJV)

Laura Burgess

Times

A time to weep, a time to laugh, I cannot always choose
When to mourn and when to dance,
It's not within my grasp.
But this I choose despite the pain or joy that comes my way,
To worship God and bless his name
And give him all the praise.

> To every thing there is a season, and a time to every
> purpose under the heaven: A time to weep, and a time
> to laugh; a time to mourn, and a time to dance;
>
> Ecclesiastes 3:1,4 (KJV)

Laura Burgess

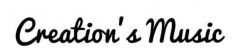

Creation's Music

Listen! Can you hear it?
The music of the spheres,
The heavenly sound of trees and hills,
The melody of the fields.
Join the chorus and praise the Lord,
Who made this glorious land,
And you may hear the hilarious sound
Of trees that clap their hands!

> For ye shall go out with joy, and be led forth with peace:
> the mountains and the hills shall break forth before you
> into singing, and all the trees of the field shall clap their
> hands.
>
> Isaiah 55:12 (KJV)

Laura Burgess

Speechless

I kneel and bow in awestruck wonder
Before my Lord and Savior.
Sovereign, Just, Almighty, Love, Unlimited Creator.
And yet he died to save my soul,
Too much to comprehend.
And so I bow and worship him, his worth will never end.

> Therefore, since we are receiving a kingdom that cannot be shaken, let us be thankful, and so worship God acceptably with reverence and awe, for our God is a consuming fire.

> Hebrews 12:28–29 (NIV)

Laura Burgess

The Promise

The promise came—the olive leaf,
Borne by God's own dove.
His faithfulness put on display and carried by his love.
Thus, to us, he sends his promise—
In me, this too shall end.
Abide in me, watch for my dove,
On me you can depend.

> And the dove came in to him in the evening; and, lo, in
> her mouth was an olive leaf pluckt off: so Noah knew
> that the waters were abated from off the earth.
>
> Genesis 8:11 (KJV)

Laura Burgess

Blinded

Peering through the fog that swirls, I try to see my way,
Immanuel, God with us, I sense him in this place.
And this I know—he's never leaving, always holding true,
So I rest in him and trust his love, he will guide me through.

> For now we see through a glass, darkly; but then face
> to face: now I know in part; but then shall I know even
> as also I am known.
>
> 1 Corinthians 13:12 (KJV)

Laura Burgess

The Comforter

Snuffle, gruffle,
Snuggle down,
Wrap yourself in love.
Soft and cuddly,
Warm and quiet,
Peace come from above.

> And I will pray the Father, and he shall give you another
> Comforter, that he may abide with you forever;
>
> John 14:16 (KJV)

Laura Burgess

Life

The young beast skips and jumps for fun,
He knows not why he does,
But joy fills up his every pore,
His life is for the young.

But the aged too can skip and run
When God is in their heart.
His joy compels, they sing and shout,
He gives a brand new start.

> He maketh them also to skip like a calf; Lebanon and
> Sirion like a young unicorn.

Psalm 29:6 (KJV)

Laura Burgess

Bumbly, Rumbly

Bumbly, rumbly, happy dance!
Pleased to serve and take the chance.
Make the choice this task to do,
Then celebrate his joy anew!

> But now hath God set the members every one of them
> in the body, as it hath pleased him.
>
> 1 Corinthians 12:18 (KJV)

Laura Burgess

Colossus

You see, I am so lumbery,
So big and wide and tubbery,
That God exclaimed, "Good! Make more!
I'm pleased with him, there's more in store!"

> And God made the beast of the earth after his kind, and cattle after their kind, and every thing that creepeth upon the earth after his kind: and God saw that it was good.
>
> Genesis 1:25 (KJV)

Laura Burgess

Spoken

Hello and welcome to my pad!
Come sit under my vine!
We'll sing and play and share some figs,
Our God has given wine!
He's spoken peace into the land,
Given sure increase,
Watched over all his creatures here,
And caused the fear to cease.

> But they shall sit every man under his vine and under
> his fig tree; and none shall make them afraid: for the
> mouth of the LORD of hosts hath spoken it.
>
> Micah 4:4 (KJV)

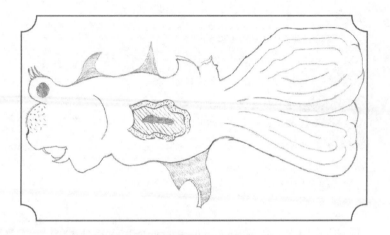

Laura Burgess

The Other View

You gaze at me with such alarm!
My looks should be amusing?
Fins and tails, skin and scales,
God made them all for using!
So don't have such a narrow view
Of God's magnificent creation,
'Cause looking up from down in here
You have quite the presentation!

> And God said, Let the waters bring forth abundantly the
> moving creature that hath life,... And God created great
> whales, and every living creature that moveth, which
> the waters brought forth abundantly,... and God saw
> that it was good.
>
> Genesis 1:20–21 (KJV)

Laura Burgess

Worship

Hallelujah, praise the Lamb!
Proclaims the angel throng.
He is worthy to be honored
And lifted up in song.
Around the throne his children come
To join the celebration,
With hands upraised and hearts in praise,
They worship him as one.

And I beheld, and I heard the voice of many angels round about the throne... Saying with a loud voice, Worthy is the Lamb that was slain to receive power, and riches, and wisdom, and strength, and honour, and glory, and blessing.

Revelation 5:11–12 (KJV)